NATURE'S PORTRAITS

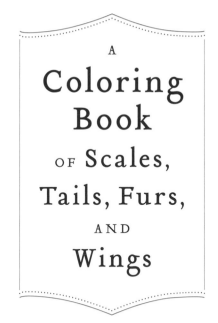

A

Coloring Book

OF Scales,

Tails, Furs,

AND

Wings

PEGGY MACNAMARA

The University of Chicago Press

CHICAGO AND LONDON

The University of Chicago Press, Chicago 60637
The University of Chicago Press, Ltd., London
© 2016 by Peggy Macnamara
All rights reserved. Published 2016.
Printed in the United States of America

25 24 23 22 21 20 19 18 17 16   1 2 3 4 5

ISBN-13: 978-0-226-43155-0 (paper)

♾ This paper meets the requirements of ANSI/NISO Z39.48–1992 (Permanence of Paper).

Easy Instructions for Using Colored Pencils

With much fear and doubt I began using color. I started with colored pencils because they felt safe. I was more comfortable with a pencil than with a brush and a wet medium. I began with a color wheel and the knowledge of three simple facts about color.

1. Colors opposite each other on the color wheel are complementary colors. They are called *complementary* because when they are placed next to each other, they complement each other—they make each other appear more vibrant. Here are the basic pairs and examples of how they might be used to take advantage of their complementary relationships:

    RED–GREEN:
    a green leaf on a red purple ground
    BLUE–ORANGE:
    an orange sunset against a blue sky
    YELLOW–VIOLET:
    a yellow daisy against a purple leaf

    When you layer complementary colors, they produce grays and browns.

2. Many species want to blend with nature so as to mimic their surroundings and keep themselves hidden from prey. So, for instance, when coloring a turtle, you could begin with red (soft parallel lines) then add a layer of green on top, and see what a beautiful gray you have created! And finally,

3. When coloring a subject that is a specific color, that color can be enhanced by using its neighboring colors on the color wheel. So, if you were painting a cardinal bright red, using a bit of orange in the light areas and some purple in the shadows would enhance the red. You subject would appear flat if you used only red.

You can learn a lot about color by observing how it works out in nature. Midday sun casts a warm yellow light and will create violet shadows. Morning light, which has a pink-orange hue, will create green-blue shadows. A blue light bulb shining on a white wall will create yellow-orange shadows. So a green leaf in the sunlight won't be green at all but a yellow-orange-green. And a shadowed leaf could have some violet. Knowing this about color makes me open to using wild color in my shadows and enables me to create rich neutrals.

Remember, there is no award for working fast. Actually, slower is better. When looking at masterpieces in a museum, you won't see any mentions of how quickly they were created. Speed is not an aspect to be considered. So take your time and enjoy!

Peggy Macnamara

Frog
{Anura}

Hedgehog
{*Erinaceidae*}

Tiger
{*Panthera tigris*}

Hyena
{*Hyaenidae*}

Cougar

{*Puma concolor*}

Red-tailed hawk
{*Buteo jamaicensis*}

Snowy owl
{*Bubo scandiacus*}

Tundra swan
{*Cygnus columbianus*}

Jaguar
{*Panthera onca*}

Turtle

{*Testudines*}

Snowy owl

{*Bubo scandiacus*}

Gyrfalcon
{*Falco rusticolus*}

Temminck's pangolin
{*Manis temminckii*}

Cannonball tree
{*Couroupita guianensis*}

Heliconia
{*Heliconia bourgaeana*}

South African honeypot
{*Protea cynaroides*}

Hummingbird
{*Trochilidae*}

American alligator
{*Alligator mississippiensis*}

Ring-necked pheasant
{*Phasianus colchicus*}

Gray fox
{*Urocyon cinereoargenteus*}

Tyrannosaurus rex

{*Tyrannosaurus rex*}

Ring-tailed lemur
{*Lemur catta*}

Blue-fronted parrot
{*Amazona aestiva*}

Moth
{*Brahmaea hearseyi*}

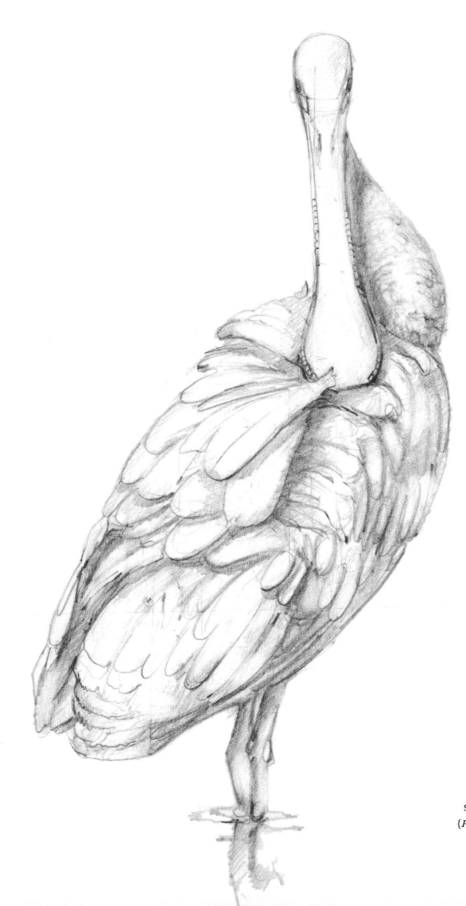

Spoonbill

{*Plataleinae*}

Blue jay

{*Cyanocitta cristata*}

Clouded leopard

{*Neofelis nebulosa*}

Magnificent bird of paradise
{*Cicinnurus magnificus*}

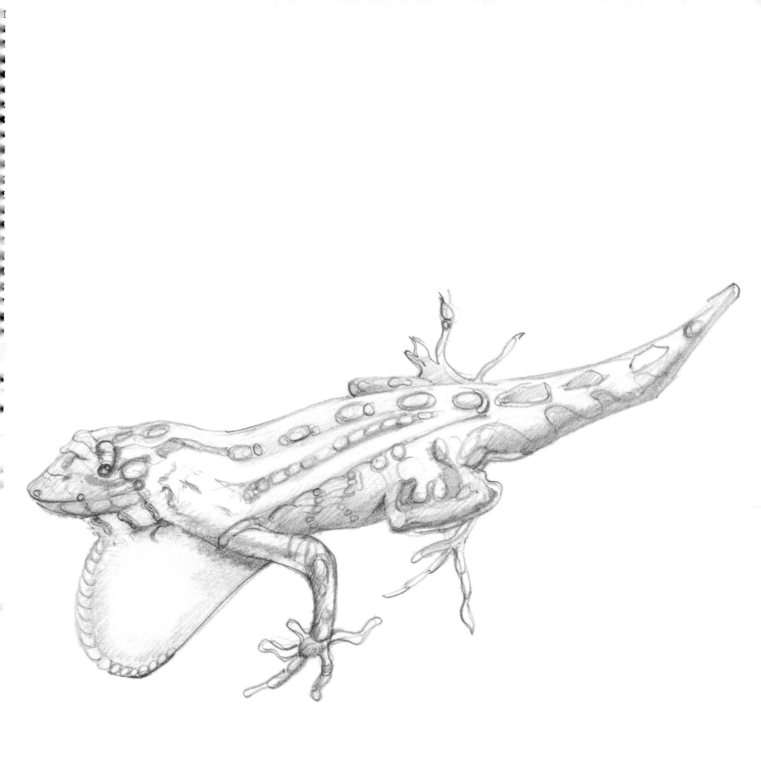

Iguanian lizard
{*Anolis*}

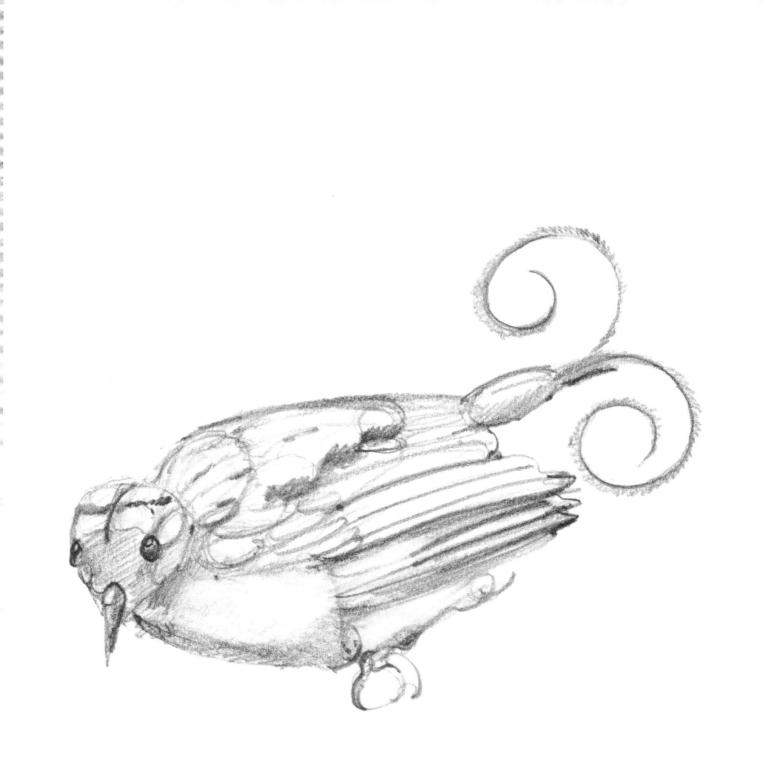

Wilson's bird of paradise
{*Cicinnurus respublica*}

African elephant
{*Loxodonta africana*}

Herrerasaurus
{*Herrerasaurus ischigualastensis*}

Ocellated turkey
{*Meleagris ocellata*}

Yellow-necked francolin
{*Francolinus leucoscepus*}

Chilean flamingo
{*Phoenicopterus chilensis*}

Burchell's zebra
{*Equus burchellii*}

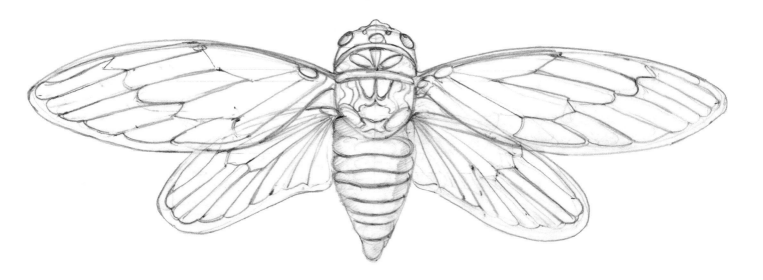

Cicada

{*Cicadidae*}

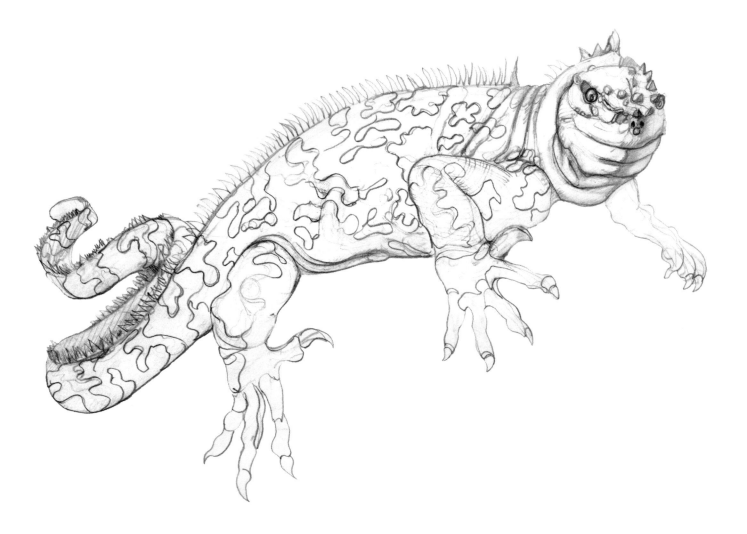

Galapagos Sea iguana

{*Amblyrhynchus cristatus*}

Leopard tortoise
{*Testudo pardalis*}

Reticulated giraffe
{*Giraffa camelopardalis reticulata*}

Coelacanth

{*Latimeria chalumnae*}

Lemur

{*Lemuroidea*}

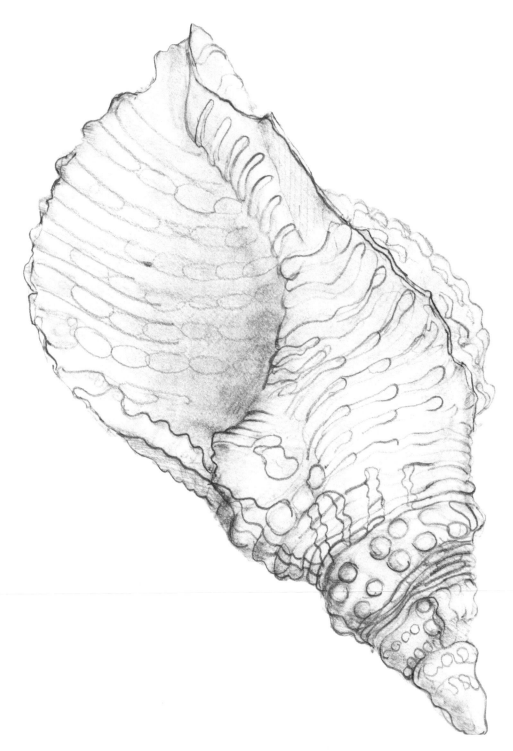

Triton's trumpets

{*Charonia nodifera*}

American flamingo
{*Phoenicopterus ruber*}

Lion

{*Panthera leo*}

Ostrich

{*Struthio camelus*}

Scarlet macaw

{*Ara macao*}

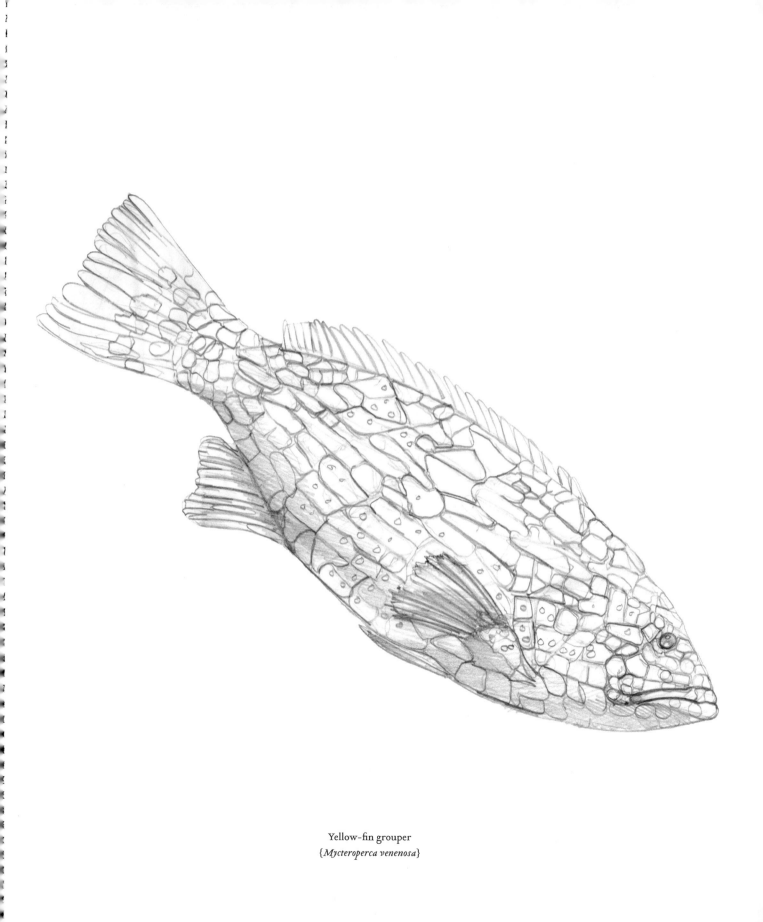

Yellow-fin grouper

{*Mycteroperca venenosa*}

Caribou
{*Rangifer tarandus*}

Peanut-head alligator bug
{*Fulgoridae*}

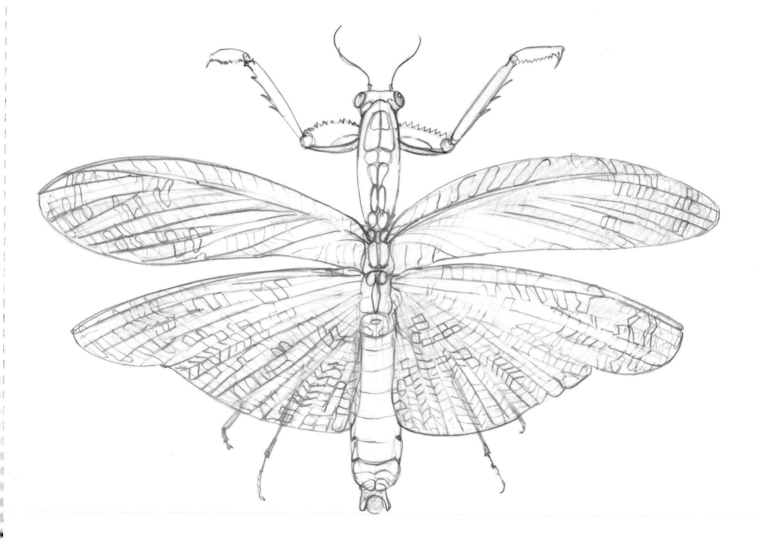

Praying mantis
{*Mantodea*}

Javanese leaf insect
{*Phyllium siccifolium*}

Lemur
{*Lemuroidea*}

Striped civit
{*Fossa fossana*}

Large katydid
{*Siliquofera grandis*}

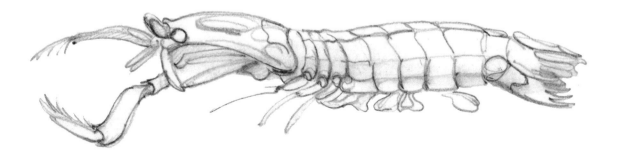

TOP Shore crab {*Grapsus strigosus*}
BOTTOM Mantic shrimp {*Squilla mantis*}

Freshwater lobster
{*Astacopsis*}

Central American caiman
{*Caiman crocodilus*}

White-winged potoo
{*Nyctibius leucopterus*}

Rat fish
{*Hydrolagus colliei*}